MEMOIRS OF AN ANXIOUS MIND

MEMOIRS OF AN ANXIOUS MIND

A collection of poems exploring Purpose, Anxiety, Depression, Suicide, Relationships and Advice from the perspective of an anxious mind.

Constantinos Kyriacou

Copyright © 2024 Constantinos Kyriacou.

All rights reserved. No part of this publication may be reproduced, distributed, or transmitted in any form or by any means, including photocopying, recording, or other electronic or mechanical methods, without the prior written permission of the author, except in the case of brief quotations embodied in critical reviews and certain other non-commercial uses permitted by copyright law.

ISBN: 978-1-3999-8609-0

Front cover image by Constantia Kyriacou
Book design by Constantinos Kyriacou

First printing edition 2024

www.mindfullcoach.com

Dedication

For every reader who finds a piece of themselves within these chapters.

Acknowledgements

This book would not have been possible without so many people present in my life. So many people who gave me and continue to give me life. So many people who help fill my cup back up when I don't have the strength to fill it up for myself.

Thank you to my talented cousin Constantia Kyriacou, who has done an absolutely incredible job with the artwork for the cover. Thank you for your time and support and for capturing this book perfectly with one image.

Thank you to my grandfather, not just for inspiring me to pick up a pen, but for providing me with a role model through your character and outlook on life. I will forever be grateful for you. Thank you also to my grandmother for keeping us all grounded and showing us what family means.

Thank you to my angel on earth, my sister. Thank you for your patience, support, advice and unconditional love. I'm so proud of the woman you have become. Thank you for being you.

Thank you to my parents for their love and support over the years. I would not be the man I am today without you both guiding me along the way. Thank you for being amazing role models and for always having my back.

Thank you to my soulmate and lead proof reader who entered my life and accepted me for who I am. Thank you for taking the time to understand me (I know that's not an easy task). Thank you for standing by my side and encouraging me along this journey. I'm forever grateful for you and us. I guess it's just a bonus that you're also an amazing cook (they do say good food is fuel for the soul).

Thank you to my cousins. You give me more life than you can imagine. It's absolute carnage when we are all together, but I love you all and wouldn't have it any other way.

Thank you to NLF. You boys are incredible, and I am forever grateful to have you all in my life.

Thank you to all the incredible people I have met at Spoken Word events over the years. Thank you for inspiring me to keep writing, to share, and to be vulnerable with my words.

Thank you to every other family member and friend I haven't mentioned above. I could fill a whole book with names and appreciations. Just know you have all had an instrumental role in moulding me into the person I am today, and for that I am forever grateful. I love you all. I appreciate you all. I can't wait to continue making memories with you guys on this journey called life.

I will leave the hardest thank you until last.

And that is a thank you to myself. Thank you for taking time to work on yourself. To understand yourself more every day. For giving yourself the opportunity to grow as a person. For giving yourself the permission to live authentically. I don't say it enough, or at all really. But I am proud of you.

Never forget that.

CONTENTS

Introducing the Author   1

01   PURPOSE from an anxious mind

Why do we live?   5
Delving Deep   6
Helping Hand   7
Dreams   8
How   9
Now   10

02   ANXIETY from an anxious mind

Anxiety   13
Facades   15
They're Looking   16
Self-Isolation   18
Voices   19
The Mind   22

03   DEPRESSION from an anxious mind

Depression   25
Him   26
Suppression   28
Be a Man   29
Cold Shoulder   31
Happy Earth Day   32

CONTENTS

04 SUICIDE from an anxious mind

The Pill	39
Wait	40
Little pick me up	41
Today is the day	42
The End	44
Don't give up	46

05 RELATIONSHIPS from an anxious mind

Views	49
It wasn't you	50
My angel	52
I'll always be alone	53
Ascension	54
State of Being	56

06 ADVICE from an anxious mind

Cope	59
Therapy	60
Fight or Flight	61
Happiness	62
Sometimes	63
Life Hacks	64

About the Author — 69
Connect with the Author — 71

Introducing the Author

The poems within this book are snapshots of my life.

Writing them came naturally, and to be honest it was the easy part. The hardest part has been to pluck up the courage to share them with the world.

These poems were not written for a book. Every piece has been something I've written for myself. To help me through difficult times. To help me through good times. To help me make sense of my world. But I truly believe the words within these pages can help someone out there.

Like so many others, I've spent my life struggling with anxiety. Falling in and out of the depths of depression. Being faced with that suicidal voice within when there seemed to be no way out. But putting thoughts onto a page has been and continues to be one of the most therapeutic processes I go through.

I first delved into the world of poetry in 2017, all thanks to my grandfather. After finding out he was an avid poet himself (and continues to write), I decided to pick a pen up myself, and haven't put it down since.

Now, the poems you are about to encounter have been arranged to help you navigate your way through an anxious mind. Read them in order, or dip in and out of them as you please. Read them aloud or quietly within. Read them in a way that makes sense for that own little voice in your head.

I hope they help you make sense of your world.

C. Kyriacou

01
PURPOSE
from an anxious mind

Why do we live?

Why are we alive, and placed on this earth?
It's a thought many of us have, from the time of our birth.

Is life all about money, and stacking up our wealth?
Even if it's at the expense, of our own mental health?
Even if it's at the expense, of our own sense of self?
I mean it's okay if it means we continue to stack money on that shelf.

Or is life all about family
and those people we meet?

The friends that are around us
and those small interactions on the street?

Don't get me wrong
money is unfortunately
a necessity we all need to live.

But even without money
there is so much more
each and every one of us
can still give.

Delving Deep

I've thought about this vividly
the reason for our birth.
The reason for our existence
and our place upon this earth.

What makes us so deserving
of our comforts, warmth and air?
When so many around us
are simply living in despair.

What is the true meaning of life?
What should we achieve?
Is there a higher being in life?
Who should we believe?

Now thoughts like this are damaging
they've often kept me down.
When approached with the wrong mindset
and a constant frown.

There's no place on this earth for me
what do I have to give?
If there's nothing I can offer people
then why should I still live?

But I've needed to go through my lowest points
to really understand.
That everyone has a role to play
to give the upper hand.

Helping Hand

Behind every success is a hardship
that someone's had to face.
Everyone goes through tough times
and even the happiest can relate.

Don't envy others for what they have
or the position they're currently in.
Who knows what goes on behind closed doors
or the battles they fight within.

Just use the arsenal of tools you have
and the cards you've been dealt.
To do something for others
that for generations will still be felt.

That's what life's about really
helping others with all you can.
And being someone who's always willing
to just lend a helping hand.

Dreams

The alarm goes off again
and I put it back on snooze.
Why do I need to wake up each day
to live a life I didn't choose?

The drive to work is hectic
thoughts running through my head.
I just want to turn around back home
and sink into my bed.

I wish I could live out my dream
but I know it's far too late.
I need to save for my future family
to put food upon their plate.

But after some time I realise
I'm not talking weeks but years.
The stress of not striving for my dreams
is not worth all these tears.

If I don't take a leap of faith now
I'll always have this regret.
And the mind is a powerful tool
something like this it will never forget.

So next time my alarm goes off
I won't put it back on snooze.
For every day is a rehearsal
for the dream that I can choose.

How

How will I know what it is in life
that I'm supposed to do?
When every day I'm winging it
I really have no clue.

How am I supposed to enjoy my life
when I seem to have no plan?
When every day I have to force a smile
and convince myself I can.

How will I ever be able to take the risks
I know will set me on my way?
When negativity always returns
to consume my thoughts in every way.

But after some time it hits me
no one's life is set in stone.
You have to trust the timing of life
and wait for your path to be shown.

Now this process may happen quickly
but for others it may take years.
Learning to fight those negative thoughts
and wipe back all those tears.

For its only at your lowest points
you really understand.
Who it is you're supposed to be
and achieve on the other hand.

So next time you seem confused
about who you are and where to go.
Just remember to trust the timing of life
and before long it will show.

Now

Past decisions and memories I delve into
every now and then.
Thinking why I made such decisions
even when I was ten.

That car, that promotion, that relationship
will set me on my way.
A better future for me I dream
and every night I pray.

But things will never make me
and achievements will come and go.
It's about living in the present moment
which will really make me feel whole.

There's no such thing as a future
and no such thing as a past.
For everything happens in the now
and life moves by way too fast.

So enjoy every day
every breath
every step that you take.

For when you enjoy this moment

all the rest

will simply

fall into place.

02
ANXIETY
from an anxious mind

Anxiety

That's it now, it's over
you're stuck with this for life.
But being diagnosed with a
Generalised Anxiety Disorder
just doesn't seem too right.

For everyone has anxiety
at some point during their week.
It's just for me, it's like my anxieties
are on a constant repeat.

Constantly fighting rumination
and playing out scenarios in my head.
Thinking and overthinking
over small things that have been said.

Now it's taken some years
for me to really understand.
That a lot of how I feel
is really in my own hands.

A big step for me was acceptance
on those days that I feel low.
And I've stopped being ashamed
of letting my true emotions show.

Who really cares what others think?
I know I no longer do.
The most important thing for your mental health,
is to concentrate on you.

Now this might sound a bit selfish
and at times it will feel this way.
You have to set aside time for yourself
to help keep your anxieties at bay.

For anxieties stem from somewhere
they all have their roots.
It's about learning about your catalysts
and controlling your thoughts.

Facades

So I will continue to strive
to be the best me.
And if anyone ever tries to contest me
I won't mind.
They can't see what I'm feeling inside
they're emotionally blind.

I've been putting up barricades around my soul for so long
I feel like I've run out of bricks.
Or maybe it's just the cement around this facade
that seems to be loosening its grip.

But whatever the reason
I feel like I'm ready to break down this wall.
Stop placing so much emphasis on other people's opinions
and within myself just stand tall.

Because fighting battles that no one sees
can often leave you feeling drained.
And it wasn't until I started wearing my vulnerability
from within on my sleeve
that I realised deep down we're all the same.

But who knows what tomorrow may bring
I may just retreat back into my shell.
Trying to put back up the walls I just broke down myself

who can really tell?

They're Looking

Everybody's looking
I feel their eyes piercing my skin.
I sit there with my eyes open
but everything's closed within.

What are they thinking about me?
Things they say behind my back.
Why is it so hard to make conversation?
So much confidence I do lack.

I try hard to make contributions
to the things that are being said.
But every time I go to speak
I get mad thoughts rushing through my head.

"Don't say that! Be quiet!
It's better if you didn't speak at all.
Every time you do open your mouth
you make us look like a fool."

So I sit and listen to my thoughts
as people joke and laugh around.
But what's strange is I can't hear a thing
there simply is no sound.

Why do I feel like this?
Where has it come from?
I'm usually not this way.
Ever since my thoughts started spiralling
I feel more isolated every day.

Now the feelings above are not depression
but they can lead to this downward trend.
This is anxiety at its finest
and it's rules you can learn to bend.

The first step is acceptance
    listening to your thoughts and how you feel.
    Inevitably some days may go just like this
    but in time you will heal.

The second step is to acknowledge
    that most your thoughts aren't actually real.
    How often do you live inside your own mind
    with thoughts that never actually reveal?

The third step is to remember,
    that we all have an individual voice.
    Turning down that conversation of self-doubt within
    I'm not saying it's an easy choice.

But thoughts only become real
once we place meaning on their construction
And if we're not careful about what we think
it can lead to devastating, internal self-destruction.

So in order for the best version of yourself to function, REMEMBER:

Have confidence in yourself.
You are unique.
No one really cares what you say.

They're not judging.
They're not thinking about you.
They're just going about their day.

Self-Isolation

We're being told to self-isolate
but I've been self-isolating for years.
Living inside my own mind on most days
often fighting back a few tears.

But people never noticed the signs in me
I practiced social distancing in my head.
And yes, there were definitely moments in my life
where I thought I would be better off dead.

But without going through those low points
I wouldn't be where I'm at now.
Being able to empathise and spot signs in others
because I know how.

Your mind can take you to dark places
and often leave you feeling estranged.
I know how hard it can be sometimes
just to be inside your own brain.

If you asked me looking back now
if I would change anything
the answer would be NO.

You can't always experience the highs
because in everybody's book of life
there's going to be chapters
of lows.

Voices

Trying to put pen to paper
as I sit down to write.
But with my own mind
I have to constantly fight.

That voice of self-doubt
that always seems to creep back.
Any confidence in my own abilities
I constantly lack.

And this voice doesn't just appear
when I try to put poetry onto a page.
I've had to live with this voice
since I was a young age.

Imagine what I could achieve without it
if I had a little more self-belief.
The weight that would be lifted off my shoulders
with a deep breath of relief.

But that voice is always present
it's constantly there.
Forcing me to doubt myself
and with others to compare.

Where does this voice come from?
I mean does everyone have their own?
Even with a mind full of thoughts
sometimes I still feel so alone.

At times it's kind to me
and at other points it drags me all the way down.
I might be smiling on the outside
but inside I feel the frown.

But each anxiety I feel can only exist
if I let that thought persist.
It's not about blocking out my thoughts
or trying to resist.

It's about accepting my thoughts
and acknowledging they're there.
And I have to stop believing that voice that tells me
it's just not fair.

Because we're all blessed in more ways than one
with every breath that we breathe.
And if you self-doubt as much as me
then you need to tell yourself, I believe.

I BELIEVE I can live my life
in conjunction with this voice.
I didn't choose to have anxiety
but how I react to it is my choice.

I BELIEVE God gave us all the power
to overcome depression.
Learning to live with your own mind
is one of the biggest life lessons.

I BELIEVE this anxiety
is almost like a gift.
Even when my body gives up
my mind puts in that extra shift.

So what I want to say to you
is accept that voice that's in your head.
Don't let it bring you down
or fill yourself with dread.

Yes, at times it may fill your mind
with an irrational fear.
And it may make your vision seem
that little less clear.

But it's a part of you
it makes you who you are.
And even if you struggle with anxiety
you can still go really far.

So pick your head up
keep moving forward
and keep working on your dreams.

Because even living with anxiety
is nothing like it seems.

The Mind

It's one of the hardest relationships in life
that you'll ever have to face.
Taking one step at a time
and building that bond at your own pace.

It feels like you've known them your whole life
but at times it feels like you don't know them at all.
Pushing your buttons at the wrong times
and driving you right up that wall.

But you make up and smile
as you get yourselves back on track.
But it's not long before they remind you
of all the confidence you still lack.

"You're a nobody. You won't survive.
You'll be nothing without me.
Just make sure you keep me close
that's the only way you'll feel free."

People say you should end it
that you deserve more respect.
But you're afraid of cutting it off now
and living with regret.

Now all the above is not a reference to the relationship
with another human kind.
It's a reference to the relationship we all have
with our own individual mind.

The power it holds over us is real
but it's just a muscle at the end of the day.
Which means you can train it to help you think
in a certain kind of way.

03
DEPRESSION
from an anxious mind

Depression

People talk about depression
like it's another form of oppression.
But maybe it's just another means
of some deeper level expression.

Or lack of
because it just leaves you feeling numb.
Sucking the life out of everything you do
just extracting all the fun.

Or maybe depression is the body's way
of telling you to slow down.
A reminder to take control of your mind again
and root your feet into the ground.

I know that it's a dark time
and you often can't see any light.
And many of your thoughts during this period
might give you a real fright.

But trust me when I tell you
there is light at the end of the tunnel.
We all have the ability to make it through hard times
and even you can switch up your own channel.

I'm not saying it's going to be easy
but with all the things you learn on the way.
You'll be able to look back and be grateful
that you decided to stay.

Him

To him it's just a game
playing with my mind.
An easy target for him
he always seems to find.

He always seems to be there
to put me in my place.
Lurking like a puff of smoke
all up in my face.

At night I close my eyes
praying that he'll go.
But in the morning he's still there
he always seems to show.

He follows me constantly
like a hovering dark cloud.
I turn to look him in the face sometimes
and he smiles oh so proud.

What does he want from me?
What have I done?
I question every day.
My whole life he seems to have taken
and he's here to stay.

But one day it seems to click
and I look all around.
He has no physical presence
so how can he be so profound?

That's when I realise I'm living
in the past and future
with my overthinking mind.

An easy target for him
he'll never ever find.

Suppression

I can see how easy it is for me
to fall into that dark hole of abyss.
Falling back into depression is still my biggest fear
and not a place I miss.

I can feel myself slipping
but I'm trying to take control.
Keeping up routines, finding strength within
and trying to keep my mind whole.

But I'm angry with myself, I can't lie
because even after all these years
I'm being hard on my own mind daily
for constantly shedding tears.

Now tears I know
are one of the best ways to get emotions out and let go.
But I'm fighting with a voice within to bury them deep
and keep them on the low.

Even after all I've learnt about my own mind
how can I let myself slip?
Is this how it's going to be my whole life?
Or is it just a temporary blip?

But as I write these words, I'm realising again
just how much control I possess.
Over my emotions and thoughts
and that negative voice I can suppress.

Be a man

I've had this voice inside my head
ever since I were small.
Is it God talking or is it the devil
I really had no clue.

But as I've grown and gone through life
I've come to the realisation.
These thoughts and voices that I heard
were just my subconscious imagination.

Overthinking and constantly falling
into that black hole of my mind.
Struggling with anxiety and being prone to depression
was just something I had to find.

Constantly feeling different, never fitting in
was I the only one who felt this way?
Throwing myself into work and studies
hoping my thoughts would stay at bay.

But it wasn't until my twentieth year
that I realised I was a sufferer.
Imagine being a slave to your mind all that time
and convincing yourself you're a nutter.

Around five depressive episodes
suicidal thoughts and attempts, and six years later.
It's taken that time to accept who I am
and stop being such a self-hater.

For I had this voice that told me
I was supposed to be a man.
Men aren't supposed to feel like this
or be as emotional as I am.

But now I realise, a real man
is forgetting how you're supposed to be perceived.
A real man is one who is accepting, opens up
and can be honest about the help they need.

Cold Shoulder

8 months of therapy and I feel like regression.
Ruminating daily, as I toy with depression.

Overthinking consumes me, imposter syndrome's at large.

How long can I keep up this sinking facade?

I'm on the edge.
I can feel it.
I'm close to falling in.

Holding on for dear life, as that dark cloud begins to spin.

But I've never been at a point where I can literally spot it on the horizon.
Which means the power is still in me to make sure that I rise on.
And soar above that cloud, before it has a chance to suck me in.
This self-doubting voice of mine will never fully win.

I have too much fight inside me, I'm a survivor above all else.
So I'm pressing that button and resetting my own mental health.

Through routines, therapy, and just easing that pressure
Of those internal metrics, and the comparisons I put on myself to measure.

And yes, medication may be necessary, if I feel that it's right.
I will get through this and be stronger for it, my future is still bright.

And that dark cloud may try to ease its way back at some point when I'm older.
But until it gets the message
I will continue to give it

the cold shoulder.

Happy Earth Day

It's been 28 years
that I've been on this earth.
But I still can't seem to celebrate
the time of my own birth.

There just always seems to be a dark cloud
that consumes me at this time of year
And as January 3rd approaches
I'm filled with anxiety and fear.

For family passings around my birthday
have been a recurring trend.
And suicidal thoughts on my 21st
had me smiling for pretend.

Maybe I've just become accustomed
in association with this date.
To portray it with mourning, a loss of life
and a sense of general self-hate.

Even while I sit here on my birthday
writing these words.
I can feel tears starting to form
and to me it seems absurd.

Because I'm still here living, breathing
and should be thankful for my life.
Deep down I know I am
but something doesn't seem too right.

My head feels heavy and clouded
and I just want to be alone.
Spend the day with myself and my thoughts
and just switch off my phone.

But I know this wouldn't be a healthy way
for me to spend my day.
For I've learnt far too much about mental health
and my own mind over the years
to know that for me
this wouldn't be okay.

Because I'll probably just sit and ruminate
over past years and the ones ahead.
Overthinking, ending up in tears
and just retreating to my bed.

So after the past few years
I've made a conscious effort instead.
To spend time with close friends and family on this day
rather than alone in my own head.

Yes, even at this grown age
it's still a difficult time for me to endure.
And if you asked me to pinpoint its exact root cause
I wouldn't be too sure.

But what I am sure about
is that there are plenty of people
who are thankful I was born.
I'm not saying you should be big headed
or blow your own horn.

But what I am trying to say
is that you need to appreciate
the positive effect you have on people's lives.
Even without you actually knowing it
you are someone's shining light.

So these next few words are a reminder for you
as much as they are a reminder for me.
We all deserve to be born
to help set each other free.

We all deserve to be born
to help each other see.
That nothing worthwhile in life comes easy
or is ever free.

Even for you to be sitting here today
a woman had to sacrifice nine months.
Share her body and her soul with you
and carried you on her front.

You see she never carried you from behind
maybe this was God's intention.
You grew as part of your mum
as her bodily extension.

The growth of a child isn't hidden
it's put forward for the world on show.
No one comes into this world alone
we needed help to grow.

Maybe that's why birthdays are so special
because when we're singing that song
we're not just celebrating an individual being
we're celebrating a very special bond.

A bond, that at one time
a cord had your bodies connected.
An umbilical kind of relationship
the kind that can't be contested.

So on my next birthday
I don't want to blow out candles for fun.
I want to blow candles with that special woman in my life
that person I call mum.

And if you take only one thing away from this poem
on your next Earth Day
I don't want you to have your head held low.

I want you to use it as a day to celebrate the life you've lived
and all the time you still have left

to grow.

04
SUICIDE
from an anxious mind

The Pill

The stigmatism that surrounds them
makes it hard for me to take.

I don't need them.

I'll be fine.

Just please give me a break.

But I know I need to do something
I'm falling deeper into descend.

As suicidal thoughts consume me

I can no longer pretend.

Wait

I'm going to do it.

I don't care.

It's the only way I see out.

No one will ever miss me.
For this I have no doubt.

Deep down I know it's wrong
the things I'm researching online.
But this will only be a temporary pain
and after things will be just fine.

But think about your family.
The amount of grief you'd put on their plate.
Even worse if you didn't do it properly
and you're left in an even more helpless state.

I don't care about that now
I'm sick of living in my own head.
The only way I can see peace for me
is if I were simply dead.

But it's getting late now
and I'm getting tired
maybe I'll just hold on.

And wait until the morning
as I listen to this song.

Little pick me up

Thoughts in your mind.

Constantly on the grind.

Pick yourself up.

Don't leave old lessons behind.

Life's all about learning, and discovering your truth.

You might be pushed to the edge sometimes

But don't jump off that roof.

Today is the day

Today is the day
I've decided that it's time.
Waiting for everyone to leave for work
reassuring them I'll be fine.

I hear the front door close
and the cars drive off
as I lay there in my bed.
Just taking some time to gather my thoughts
with these demons in my head.

Finally forcing myself to get up
with my bare feet touching the ground.
There's no place for you, you have to do it
you can't turn this around.

So I go downstairs and grab a bag
as I place it over my head.
Squeezing as tight as I can to block out the air
hoping that I'll be dead.

But I begin to panic, as tears start rushing
I quickly rip it off.
Gasping for air, and clutching my throat
as I frantically begin to cough.

Now this isn't the first time I've attempted this
it was only the other week.
That I tied a band around my squat rack to hang myself
but of this I never speak.

Looking back today, I can appreciate
the effect depression has on your mind.
Unable to think clearly, having tunnel vision
to that darkness that's behind.

But if I can make it onto the other side
then trust me you can too.
Just be open about asking for help
and talking these things through.

The End

I'm no good.
My world is bleak.
My future is hopeless.

Thoughts that run in my head.

Maybe people would be much happier
if only I were dead.

"STOP!"
My other half shouts
"Why think such thoughts at all?
If anyone knew the things you're thinking
they'd think you were a fool."

But around family I feel like a stranger
and to friends I don't exist.
The reasons I should end my life
I can compile on a list.

Around train tracks I feel nervous
for the actions I may take.
Why not just end it here and now
for everybody's sake.

My life flashes before me
every decision I have made.
I can't live a future with all these thoughts
and to my mind remain a slave.

STOP! There are people who love you
you know that this is true.
Your mum, your dad, your sister
would do anything for you.

Don't be a slave to your mind
it can be a devil with this game.
These negative thoughts and emotions you feel
you need to learn to tame.

So don't be ashamed to get the help you need
to set you on your way.
And before long you will start
to see the good in every day.

For depression is an illness
and anxiety and suicide are real.
But you can start by taking a small step each day

by saying how you feel.

Don't give up

I know how hard it can be
to just get out of bed.
With overpowering thoughts constantly spinning
and messing with your head.

I know how it feels
to think you just don't belong.
Getting emotional over the smallest things
thinking it would be better if you were gone.

I know how it is
to feel like you're not even alive.
But still feeling your heart beating
with no clue as to how you're going to survive.

I know how it goes
to be in a room of people, but feel so alone.
Being surrounded by friends and family
but still feeling like you're in a silent zone.

But don't give up on yourself now
you need to be your number one fan.
Take one day at a time
and just do the things you can.

They say time is the biggest healer
and trust me when I say it really is.
Just find that courage to keep yourself
going long enough to see
why you should still live.

05
RELATIONSHIPS
from an anxious mind

Views

I can't expect everyone
to think as I do.
What goes on in my mind
people just have no clue.

Frustration I often feel
when I put other's feelings first.
But the same acts of kindness
are not received in reverse.

Often wishing that someone
could see the world from my view.
But everyone has their own window
that they're looking through.

It wasn't you

When you read that poem to me
blaming yourself for my mind.
I just sat there and listened
blocking tears from behind.

Even writing these words
is so hard for me to do.
Feeling myself well up inside
I thought these feelings were through.

Maybe it is hereditary
no one really knows for sure.
But the thought of you blaming yourself
sinks my heart to the floor.

If you're still sitting there thinking
all this was your fault.
Then I want to say thank you
for the gifts that you brought.

Thank you
    for my anxiety
    that I live with every day.
    Yes I may over analyse
    but it helps me think in a certain way.

Thank you
    for putting me through depression
    and all that it taught.
    I'm now able to empathise with people
    when they have that dark thought.

Thank you
   for providing me with the strength
   to keep myself alive.
   I will never underestimate the power the mind has
   to help you to survive.

Thank you
   for carrying me for 9 months
   all the stress I put your body through.
   Don't blame yourself for what you think you gave me.

It really wasn't you.

My Angel

Through blood we're considered family
but my life angel you are to me.
Pushing me through tough times
and helping me feel free.

Now I know it's not been easy
to watch me descend along the years.
As I delve in and out of depression
I know I've cost you many tears.

Frustration you've no doubt felt
as you attempt to pick me off my knees.
But that black hole of self-doubt and destruction
I seem to fall into with ease.

But you've been patient
even if you don't know
exactly how I feel.

Just talking through and advising me
you've helped my soul to heal.

The things I've achieved, and where I'm at
you're the reason I'm still alive.
Opening up about suicidal thoughts and attempts
you've helped me to survive.

I want you to know I'm here for you
as you always are for me.

Through blood we're considered siblings
but my life angel you are to me.

I'll always be alone

How
can I ever commit
to another human soul?

When I don't even know myself, which direction my mind will go.

How
can I ever be strong enough
to let somebody in?

To a world of ups and downs, with my mind in a constant spin.

How
can I ever expect anyone
to really understand?

To live life filled with anxiety, and be prone to depression on the other hand.

How
can I ever be confident
to let someone know how I feel?

With a fear of being judged, it's just not worth the big reveal.

How
can I ever expect someone
to take on all my burdens?

It's just not fair, and so much easier, to just close my inner curtains.

Ascension

Falling in love kind of sounds
like you're always descending.
But with you my wings soar
everyday I'm ascending.

Taking us to new heights
that's not to say there hasn't been lows.
But without a few tears
true love can never really grow.

Because tears show vulnerability
a part that people often hide.
And I'm not oblivious to the fact
that relationships also have a bumpy side.

But it's overcoming these bumps
that makes you both whole.
Talking through, and communicating
and letting your true intentions show.

But at times it's hard for me
being such a chronic overthinker.
Letting rumination take over
as some thoughts begin to linger.

Now I know thoughts aren't reality
I can't let the dark side win.
Seeing the real me, but at times
I want to keep those curtains closed within.

Because I trust you with my life
my body and my soul.
It's just at times I find it hard
to let my mind fully go.

I just don't want to burden you
with all the things that are in my head.
And at times I think it's easier
if I just keep them in instead.

I'm supposed to be the man in the relationship
constructed by society's point of view.
Remaining strong, suppressing emotion
and never feeling blue.

Now the things above aren't actually anything
you've ever made me feel,
You can read my aura and my mood
with you I'm not afraid to be real.

But they're still thoughts that linger
at times when I'm feeling low.
I'm just so glad that with you
I'm not afraid of letting my true emotions show.

Sharing our thoughts and feelings
is how we'll keep this relationship strong.
I know you're the one I'm meant to be with
there's such a strong sense that we belong.

It's a comfort of feeling at home
whenever you're in my presence.
Building branches off these roots
you've become a true part of my essence.

State of Being

Is love an emotion
or a state of being?
A bubble of contentment
as your soul keeps freeing.

It's a state of being
with emotions attached.
Where two become one
as both souls become latched.

Where emotions intertwine
there's both lows and highs.
There's days where you smile
and days where you cry.

But through it all
one thing about love is for sure.
Whatever they feel
you also feel in your core.

Because love isn't an emotion
it's a state of being.
A joint bubble of contentment
where both souls keep freeing.

06
ADVICE
from an anxious mind

Cope

I keep looking for one
but there's multiple ways to cope.

It's about implementing a few mechanisms
to make sure you don't choke.

Whether that's exercise, writing,
or finding a new way to think.

Rewiring your way of thinking
so your mental health doesn't sink.

And even if you've sunk down slightly
it doesn't mean that you've failed.

It means working harder on your mind now
to make sure you prevail.

Living with anxiety is still living
you can still spread your wings and prosper.

Just take time to quieten that voice
that tells you you're an imposter.

Therapy

Therapy isn't something you just go to as a last resort.

And unfortunately dealing with your mental health
isn't something the youth are currently taught.

Therapy is a place to go to learn how to cope.
To deal with trauma, and learn new ways to steady that anxiety rope.

To learn about your mind, and the intricacies below.
To open yourself up to the other side of vulnerability
and let your voice inside show.

And mental health struggles don't discriminate against any one gender.
Men in particular shouldn't have to keep it all in and simply surrender.

Keeping it bottled up inside until it's too late.
Only asking for help once they've reached heaven's gate.

We need to make that gate available here on Earth.
Make a haven for men to be able to root themselves into this turf.

To speak freely about their troubles, anxieties and woes.
Not having to wait until they're on the cliff's edge

hanging on by their toes.

Fight or Flight

You don't always have to know
exactly what it is in life
you're supposed to do.
Sometimes you just have to wait,
be patient, and see things through.

Now I'm not saying every opportunity
will just come straight your way.
But with every sunrise, comes with it a new day.

Which means everyone has new opportunities
to learn and grow.
New opportunities to reinvent yourself
and for your best version to show.

Take time to write your goals down
with the things you want to achieve.
And be careful with the things you hear
and all the things you believe.

There will no doubt be hard moments in your life
that you're going to have to endure.
And there will be opportunities that come your way
that you simply can't ignore.

So make sure you take the risk
when you know deep down it feels right.

Push your anxieties down
and remember
it's just a false alarm

of fight or flight.

Happiness

Happiness can be an emotion
but it's also a state of mind.
It's about accepting your present state
and those blessings you can find.

Don't wait for happiness to emerge
in that future you say you see.
Just be grateful for what you have in life
and let your mind be free.

Now I'm not saying you should be happy
every hour of every day.
For there will be moments in your life
that will set you off your way.

But it's important to make a conscious effort
to the way that you react.
To things that happen around you
don't take negativity as a simple matter of fact.

It's important not to place your happiness
in that possession, person or promotion.
For when you can't be happy with yourself
you will always bring negativity into motion.

So take a moment to contemplate
all things in your life that are worthwhile.

And remember that a frown uses up more
energy and muscles

than a simple smile.

Sometimes

Sometimes
you need to get away, to clear your mind.
Recentre your soul, and take in the sun's shine.

Sometimes
you need to see the world in a different setting.
To be reminded of all the simple intricacies of life you keep forgetting.

Sometimes
you need to travel to help refocus your brain.
Breathing in some fresh air, helping you mentally reframe.

Sometimes
you need to get away, from that race of modern living.
To put yourself first, and stop constantly giving.

Sometimes
you have to force yourself, to just be alone.
Spend time with your thoughts, and put down your phone.

Sometimes
you have to take a step back, and reconnect with your soul.
To remind yourself of all the things in life that truly matter

and that make you feel whole.

Life Hacks

Everyone's melody of life
takes the sound of different tones.
And living in your own mind
can often lead to an extremely silent zone.

But don't replay scenarios, over and over
of things that have been said.
Keep them frozen in the past
and just release them from your head.

It's okay to say goodbye to the old you
and let in a new awakened spirit.
A fresh page to start on
and a new lease of life to exhibit.

The key to really unlock life is simple
and deep down we know it's true.
Focus on living in this present moment
with this new awakened you.

Sitting here as I look at the
views all around.

There was a time when I
never thought, I'd still have
my feet on the ground.

For it's taken some time, to
open my eyes and really see.

How proud I should be of
myself, for just being me.

About the Authour

Constantinos Kyriacou (also known as Mindfull Coach), is a London based Spoken Word Poet.

He uses poetry as a tool to help him make sense of his own mind and navigate his way through life. His motivation for writing stems from his experiences of battling depression, suicide and a lifetime of anxiety.

Since 2017, he has found the courage to speak openly about such topics, and through his poetry, wants to encourage others to do the same. Memoirs of an Anxious Mind is his first solo publication.

Constantinos has performed and headlined across a number of open mic events over the years (including the Backyard Comedy Club), had work published in the Words By anthology which launched in 2019 and featured in the rap duo Kings Cvstle's 2022 EP Enroute.

After qualifying as a chartered accountant, Constantinos decided to take the plunge to start his own business. With a lifelong passion for fitness (which has also been an instrumental tool in helping him manage his mental health), he set out to create his own fitness studio which opened in 2021, with the aim of putting the MIND back into fitness. Taking the emphasis off of just what you look like and back into focussing on how you FEEL.

Today, Constantinos continues to build his business as a Personal Trainer in his private North London studio. He employs a holistic, individualised approach to empower individuals to strengthen their body & mind by creating healthy, sustainable habits around movement, intuitive eating & intentional daily routines.

Constantinos is also an Online Coach, a Group Exercise Class Instructor for Corporate Firms, a Poet and Workshop Facilitator and a Motivational Speaker.

MINDFULL COACH
LIVE. MOVE. CREATE.

Connect with the Authour

Connect with Constantinos on Instagram
@mindfullcoach

For any business related enquiries,
contact Constantinos via email at
info@mindfullcoach.com

For more information, visit
www.mindfullcoach.com

Mental Health Helplines

If you need to talk right now, there are many helplines staffed by trained people ready to listen. They won't judge you, and could help you make sense of what you're feeling.

Many listening services let you talk for as long as you need. This page lists some options to try.

Samaritans
To talk about anything that is upsetting you, you can contact Samaritans 24 hours a day, 365 days a year. You can call **116 123** (free from any phone), email **jo@samaritans.org** or visit some branches in person.

SANEline
If you're experiencing a mental health problem or supporting someone else, you can call SANEline on **0300 304 7000** (4.30pm–10pm every day).

National Suicide Prevention Helpline UK
Offers a supportive listening service to anyone with thoughts of suicide. You can call them on **0800 689 5652** (6pm to midnight every day).

Campaign Against Living Miserably (CALM)
You can call the CALM on **0800 58 58 58** (5pm–midnight every day) if you are struggling and need to talk. Or if you prefer not to speak on the phone, you could try the CALM webchat service.

Shout
If you would prefer not to talk but want some mental health support, you could text SHOUT to **85258**. Shout offers a confidential 24/7 text service providing support if you are in crisis and need immediate help.

Papyrus HOPELINEUK
If you're under 35 and struggling with suicidal feelings, or concerned about a young person who might be struggling, you can call Papyrus HOPELINEUK on **0800 068 4141** (24 hours, 7 days a week), email **pat@papyrus-uk.org** or text **07786 209 697**.

Nightline
If you're a student, you can look on the Nightline website to see if your university or college offers a night-time listening service. Nightline phone operators are all students too.

Helplines Partnership
For more options, visit the Helplines Partnership website for a directory of UK helplines.